Lockdown Latitudes

Poems 2019-2021

Steven Waling

Leafe Press

Published by Leafe Press
Nottingham, England.
www.leafepresspoetry.com

Cover photograph by Steven Waling

ISBN: 978-1-9999451-8-3

Acknowledgements:

Poems have been published in Tentacular 7, Hidden Voices, Worktown Words, International Times, Under the Baobab Tree: Poems for Madagascar, Mid-Life Crisis Zine: the Virus Edition

Thanks are due to Francesca Pridham for her invaluable editorial advice, most of which I took.

CONTENTS

LOCKDOWN LATITUDES

"And Jesus saith unto him, the foxes have holes and the birds of the air have nests, but the son of man has not anywhere to lay his head."

Mathew 8:20

These poems date from just before the pandemic to the time when the vaccine started to make a difference, and are variously about, or infected by, the circumstances both political and personal of the year of the pandemic.

Steven Waling

IN THE BOMBED-OUT CHURCH

The suddenly opened space   for the spirit
to blow in   Lord lettest now thy servant

formerly an orchard   depart in pieces
all the way down to the river   which

was closer once   wide languid silver
flows past   St Mary del Quay   patron

of sailors   if we listened to animals what
would we pray for us now and at the hour

of the night of 6th May 1941   the most
heavily bombed   outside of London

*

This was St Luke's   tune in to the choir's
gothic perpendicular   of whales & dolphins

singing   wind shrills through the falling down
house of the Lord   dedicated to slavers

ferry masters stevedores   rich & poor
travelling the Overhead Railway   please

feel free to write your comments   next
to the old docks   warehouses factories

cleared for housing   black bronzes chained
to their monuments   in municipal squares

*

This one's a bit gnarlier   it seems
waves of Nazi bombers   failed to shut

the Port of Liverpool   singing with dolphins

famished Irishmen loaded on boats   unglassed

windows of the Doctor's Church   shape of the
Rood
echoes that of an anchor   Go in peace to

love & what might we say about the state
of our planet   more or less abandoned

the past   never quite over and done with
every passion blending   burnt for three days

EYE SEA
(to my sister, Julie Cropper)

Carry this home
in the belly of your camera

Pixelate old fishing boats
then a trip up the Orme
to capture everything

Look out to sea
how calm how calm
how lovely with weather today

Move between cameras
his borrowed one and yours
to see how it affects the seen

Take a picture of the quilt
on the bed of
the smallest house in Britain
(fine example of Welsh stitching)

That 6 foot fisherman
feet out the window
head against the old town wall

find yourself in the house
of a man who knew Henry VIII
snap furniture views from windows
kitchen & tower

(in those days of course
the Welsh weren't allowed
within miles of Conwy)
You have an eye for the buoys

Move between cameras
to capture

effects of scale

And time to sit
on a bench & catch
the flight of gulls
in your big lens

They won't keep still

Wander the stony
beach for interesting lichen
barnacles stones
to bounce along waves like worries
chucked away for the day

From the stall by the pier
ozone & vinegar

Sniff the air

Go on

Sniff the air

LOCKDOWN LASSITUDE

I start to write   it all
falls apart   ink weeps down
my face   look at that view
of our car park   I like

the way   bird song enters through
the open page   I'm a plateau
staring up at the mountain
start again   A bus drawls up

the valley below   slides past with
nobody on it   keyworkers in masks
the page   is crowded with birds
and a cat enters the window

nightly to catch them out   never
seen trams so empty   the number
of dead   rises alarmingly keep your eye
on those pigeons   twitters of passerines

stuck at the top of this peak
wondering how to get down   when
Chet Baker winds through the café
I've made myself   disembodied brain

give me coffee and a square
of millionaire's shortbread   start
again   Feel my synapses buzz
up the road to base camp   find

a route no-one has trod   I
seem to like this but   Again

SPRING IN A TIME OF CONTAGION

Spring persists   An elderly man
in the supermarket   dual carriageway daffs
and a woman sanitising hands
as she descends from the bus

left with nothing   clouds stripped
sun shoves through   it'll all
be over before you know it
when the highlight of today

is buying toilet rolls   Hours
lengthen again   Finally the rain decides
to stop   old man staring
at his shopping list   wonders what

next as dolphins swim canals
Only four items of each

product   it all starts again
humanity is now closed   for unavoidable
arias on balconies   a van
shouting 'stay in your homes' at pigeons

confined under eaves   I saw parakeets
on my allotted walk   breath
keeps to itself   so who will
deliver the old man's groceries

sky so blue it hurts
I buy potatoes and a paper
with puzzles   Crack open buds
I'll try to be an optimist

as poetry makes nothing but
the swallows rejoice clean air

SCI-FI DAYZ

wherever I am
    whatever I'm from
it's not here

That shouldn't concern you clever
enthusiastic young chap   History
  of the Lancashire Cotton what   we have courses
    in Office Skills alienation

     tomorrow
  is the 70's

    on the planet
  where no one remembers
  the rain

    beam me up Scotty

from grey socks & uniform
    cobblestone hearts
    millstone shoes

beam me up

*

    From the Russo-
     Japanese War
      will butter no
    parsnips round here

no call for that
    small feet really   no call for
  father's factory   glam rock the voyage

    to my silverfoil moonbase
    with boots to match

where they quaff pink drinks
in perpetual starlight

Vermillion Sands
under the Central Pier

what is that   boy/fish/girl
what's he wearing   on her face

*

Days
when the weather changed sex
hourly

in the classroom from

the assassination of Franz
Ferdinand   to Auschwitz
and the Post-War German Miracle

from walk to school   aliens
sing   Children of the Revolution
on Top of the Pops

not much call for
Bismarck and the Entente Cordiale
in these parts I suggest
the Civil Service exams

from how are you with numbers maybe
accountancy and at the end
you'll have letters after your

ghosts of famine choirs on street corners   really

for reference only do you own
a suit solid ladder to a pension
one day these facts might

work to earn
a seat on the cloud
with your name on it

REASONABLE MEANS

This bad egg in a shell suit
I mean   my phone stopped mid
sentence   pressing buttons didn't help

Doesn't he scrub up well   I mean
sitting in his garden chair in the
Rose Garden   I just left

it what could I do   Puts on
clean shirt no tie for the camera
so I just walked home

Who lives without phones   I couldn't even
get in touch with you to say   my
phone wasn't working   My kingdom

for a payphone   The aide becomes news
at No. 10 smelling of expensive aftershave
sweating a little   hesitant   I

mean I could send lots of e-mails
but   He drove miles for his family
social distancing all the way

panic in the streets of Barnard Castle
looking for a phone-shop or degree
of insight   headless chicken wears

nice trousers   If he'd admitted to fear
would we have judged   Anyways it
started the phone I mean   at

half three in the morning   just bipped
to meditation starts at eight pm   finally slept
woke at nine   last night a text   I missed

WELCOME TO EIRE

this is the year I nearly
lose my hat   see

that pilot boat wasp past   make its
shrill announcement to the pier   no

dolphins in sight   at Dún Laorghaire
a buoy gently bobs   Bob

a boy   points at it   Wicklow
Hills   have you seen them before

when you came   searching for Yeats
That storm buckets down

Kilarney our one night under canvas
Next day sunshine   and ravens

after my sandwiches   Then Funghi
leaping the waves in Dingle Bay

nothing but glare between us and
America   Maybe a bookshop we can

buy some stolen histories   When did
sailors stop singing down gangplanks in

New York   They say
the boat trip's free if Funghi

doesn't show   he does
pleased to see us   we pay

take pictures   all over the place
past famine roads   emptied cottages

we coach to Cork where the docksides
twang like a fiddle string

cheap hostels   long conversations
I ate a lovely fish

me tourist   you traveller   split the
difference   Hours spent staring at sea

and the dolphin's philosophy of Guiness
too heavy for me   This photo
with James Joyce   wearing my hat

CREPUSCULE WITH NICA

The weight of his intelligence   in late
American twilight   stands awkward in fur coat

and hat   white gloves   Here she's with
some of her three hundred cats   Order

out of chaos   Monk's fingers jumping chords
needs someone to look after him   Her

blue Bentley by the kerb   "The most
beautiful man I ever saw"   Three wishes:

*To be an excellent musicia*n   Long shadows
of the post-war blues   her leopardskin

blowing in the breeze   They called her
the Jazz Baroness   mother to a tribe

of cats who sleep all day and
play all night   *To have a crazy*

friend like you   whose namesake's a moth
once raced Miles Davis down Fifth Avenue

her impulse to collect   paintings   musicians   cats
first time hearing Round Midnight   That time

cops took his licence   Nica took his
rap   I heard that junkie Parker died

in her apartment   "I should care   I
should go without sleeping"   Monk prowling round

the melody   Dark clubs where the cats
create havoc in the instruments   new sounds

create themselves at night   and she's home
in the halfdark streets   *A happy family*

Nica says   "Thelonius   you have that already

LOWRY'S LAMPS

"Lavishly illustrated"   we sat apart
with a milky coffee and vanilla slice

why do you never finish   "Previously
unseen"   an important aspect of

"New Road Layout for Social"
expression of solitude   Waiting

at the top of the footbridge   "Please"
mother and child   "Stand at least

2 lifetimes apart"   "I can't think why
you'd ever leave"   New perspectives

on the art   of mucky clouds   a
single man asleep on a wall   "you won't

find finer"   with all the eccentrics
old & lame   "lampposts"   gone

the way of   this creepy nostalgia
"down South"   "paint what you know"

the mills that industrial fog   tea
bread & butter   as the Irishman

leaps bollards   we're wearing our masks
down the shops   in Copson St   he

Salaam Aleichem's the owners
of Asian chicken shops   he'll do

himself an injury   so he will   "a
judicious sense of"   artistic licence

lamppost & fence   street corner solitary

won't keep the strangeness   at bay

"a man with red eyes"   too little sleep
in flat cap & visor   I almost didn't

recognise you   with your hair   cut to this
ache of return   to be transposed

to a past you've   never lived   The last
Edwardian streetlamps   replaced
by concrete posts   sodium ghosts

AUTOBIOGRAPHIA LITERARIA

I kick a ball repeatedly against the garage door. I'm taking little white pills again, only this time for blood pressure not epilepsy. The local Art Gallery has the largest Tiffany glass collection outside of the United States, so the brochure says. A poem is a machine made of language and hope. At that age, "What do you want to do with your life?" is a multiple choice question in an exam you never studied for. There's a groove in the bridge of my nose where my glasses rest.

In my Granddad's house, Thursdays are always Tripe Night. What kind of wine goes well with my first goat curry? The old bitch, our only pet dog, finds herself in the autumn of her days, having to put up with the cats running rings round her feet. I write my best work at night, fast asleep, and when I wake remember a sentence, a phrase, a random couple of words. The moon is haloed by clouds. Locked in the gallery, the pictures are coming to life.

There's a word for this feeling but I've forgotten what it is. Caution cleaning in progress. My first poem is published in the local newspaper: it concerns a horse in a field next to the power station. I sit with my mother watching Midwinter Murders, and she tells me of the lion who sleeps in a corner of her bedroom. Anything that's solid, don't kick it. On the train home we have our first taste of avocado; not impressed, but I suppose like olives it's a taste you grow into when older. Teenage kicks on the Peel Show nightly under the sheets

INTO THE WOODS

under our feet   What's scrabbling thru the
undergrowth   Roar of the motorway   Rattle
of a tram   squirrels carry fairy tales

in tiny hands   What was this place
kiss-chasing thru remnants   of ancient woods
not large enough to sustain   Kids

BMX over bumps   Someone said it was
a girls' school   nuns teaching tennis or
netball on a sunny afternoon   old

trees new growth   next to the river
bursting banks   clearly we were lost
at regular intervals   among ecosystems

built on reclaimed land   birdsnests   Then
for a while an all-weather pitch   sports
club that sort of thing   Cars thunder

over the overpass   bisecting the wild
creation of wetland   but we're never
really lost   as trees take over the old

changing rooms   wild ramsons   bluebell
ducks under shelter and a cormorant
batwinging   by the lakeside path   fish

avoid the hooks in clear water
90 foot deep in places   teal   snipe
apparently   and at least 3 heron   Boughs

hung with words   by the footpath dreams
of happy trees   sad trees   fallen trees
this the kind of place   you'd likely find

a ring or   an old sword   rising
from the lake or   by the boatyards perhaps
where the old girls play   in flooded courts

IN DEEP TIME

"Like the chameleon, keep one eye on the future
  and one eye on the past." (Malagasy proverb)

Let the dance begin   Time stretched
like a line   leads backwards
forwards   Once upon a deep

geologic interval   the Sky watched
the flux of life redrawn   overlaid
with the asking of questions

as Earth   the Self-Created
took root   everywhere   at home
in the questions   Time entered

flew through the feasthall   asked What
is this land we live in
where Sky comes down to see

what's happening and Earth
makes animals and men   of clay
but can't make them live   So

Sky speaks   Hold your breath
against Time   I will blow
life in these questions that refuse

to be answered   So beautiful
he says   their futures must be sky
but Earth said no   let their bodies

stay   and you have their souls
one stroke of a nail file   erases
their lives   let them remain

earth creatures   with heads among stars

ALLINGHAM HOUSE

What's her story   this elderly Jewess
inquisitive eyes   varicosed legs

Midsomer Murders meets Coronation Street
in a corner of the lounge   she stays up

watches everyone   What about
this old girl   wandering   where's

she going in slippers like that   Or
him in his cardigan asleep   drops in

on ladies' bedrooms   forgets
what he went there for   Meanwhile

our queen's wheeled in   in high back throne
back for coffee clogged with thickener

Two And A Half Men has her bemused
dreaming of someone   to take her

away from that woman   screaming her
head off next door   Oh help

oh help   chin up   chin up
anoint with oil and pray

to God in the flickering lightbulb   pray
for us now   and the queen of heaven

who squeezed my heart   half-hoping
that her story's not quite told

MISTER FOX'S DAILY WALK

In broad daylight Mister Fox
a line of cars behind
the learner driver speeds up
as he turns the corner

leaves turn carmine yellow crunch
crisp air underfoot the ambulance
outside the old folks home
say hello to the cats

guarding the owners' door steps
sweet aroma of lavender
passing the squeals of children
the season of leafblowers

and garden maintenance Fox squints
in bright sunlight pedestrians cross
here deep excavations magpies
rooftop rows & the cancer hospital

bus stops still green trees
new builds essential gas works
scarletting acers clear blue sky
when red light shows wait

by the telephone exchange Mister
Fox thinks is watching us rainbow
NHS we love you window
who can visit clouds clearing

helicopter undersong I wonder who
he's looking for Fox stares
straight at me tar smell
acrid dark as black molasses

SHOWERING A MAN

Saturday night, at the Metro. The whirring electric yellow of an approaching tram on the opposite platform. It's dark. A young man buys his ticket from the machine, stands five feet away looking out at the tracks. He turns his head, looks at you.

> So where you off tonight?
> Work
> This time o' night? Who starts work at 10?

You carry the heft of a body
    push, pull, heft an arm left
    heft a leg right, heft the weight of a man

You must fully engage in the dance
    push the body back on the bed
    roll it to the left, roll it to the right
    roll the body back on its back

You must fully engage in the dance
    lift an arm above the head
    move a hand into position
    turn the head to right or left

You must fully engage in the dance
    move shoulders to the middle
    lift the feet onto the plate
    shift the body by degrees

You carry the heft of a body
    until he's sitting comfortably

A half-moon over the rooftops, scattered clouds scud across the clear black sky, a few stars poke through the light pollution. You shiver in the sudden breeze.

I'm a carer. I put a man in a wheelchair to bed, get him up
    in the morning.

There it is: the Look. Eyes widen, then narrow in sympathy.
The voice softens.

That's such a good thing to do.
I know I don't get paid enough.

TEN LANCASHIRE WORDS TO BE REINTRODUCED TO THE LANGUAGE

DREE: *persistent rain*

Every day steady monotonous bored   ennui clouds coming in from the
Irish Sea   same bad news from the continent   stay bored   stay vague
protect the government

MARDY: *soft, moany*

Fed up   can't do anything   go anywhere   always moaning about this
that the days dragging on and on   Be positive like newsreaders reciting
the figures   search for the hero inside the distraction

DEGGING: *watering the flowers*

Weather favourable   spend time in the garden if you have one   dig
your potatoes and water the flowers with your grief   your soul   grow-
ing in darkness like the rhubarb in your shed   weeping silently

POWFAGGED: *exhausted*

All zoomed out   3 meetings 1 day   nights muggy with the sun up ear-
ly through blinds   Lips unsynched to the language   mazy eyed   sleep
furloughed for the next 3 months   Fogged with fake news and Facebook
the figures are rising again

MIZZLING: *drizzle*

The kind of rain that wets   drip drip   bad news drip drip   turn off
the telly drip   drip it's sunny outside   drip drp   let's go for a drp
walk in the country drp dp   everything's closed   drp dp dp out in the
world drp dp   do you know anyone dp dp pp   affected dp pp pp by
drp p ppp p Yes pp pp p   p   p   p

BAGGIN: *snack between meals*

Chocolate! How many bars?

PETTY: *toilet*

When you go one of your long walks because every day is the same and
you need to get out of the house do something just to break the routine
and the man on the telly says you have to get exercise and you need to
do something anything and you can't stand that smug git and his bloody
cycling shorts remember to find somewhere with trees   lots of trees
    You can't just pop in a pub   use the facilities   and go

MITHERED: *worried*

Wake up from dreams of unemployment lines   do you need a mask
wake up from dreams of locked-up high streets   you need a mask
numbers of cases & deaths   have you remembered your mask   wake
up from dreams of toilet paper & bread   Have you remembered your
mask   go back and pick up your mask

WAMBLY: *shaky, feverish*

Not going in there   And you may find yourself   among too many peo-
ple   outside a beautiful shop   I only want bread   in the middle of the
road   thinking   toilet paper   how did I get here   not going in there
spectacles fogged   where is my beautiful house   how did I get here
whose is that large automobile   slouching towards Barnard Castle to be
eye tested

NODDY: *idiot, fool*

Too many:

Villains   starvelings thick as a Tewkesbury mustard   sausage-faced
gammon burghers   cream-faced conspiracy loons   cockwombles
scullions, rampalians and Tumpilarians   plonkers   boil-brained barna-
cles with less sense than mutton   dickheads, wankers and pricks   sag-
bellied hugger muggers   bawbags   surly-faced anti-mask codpieces
tickle-brained & anti-vax varlets

about in the streets

be paranoid   stay paranoid   protect the paranoid

JESUS STROLLS DOWN MARKET STREET

All he wants is new underwear and a coffee in Starbucks, time to himself to phone his dad and see he's looking after himself during the lockdown. He sees they're back again on the corner of Piccadilly Gardens and Market Street, shouting his name like a weapon at random strangers. He sneaks past, hand in front of his face. He'd like to shout in their faces, ask them what the hell they thought they were doing. Not that they'd recognise who he was, and anyway, these days he just gets embarrassed, avoiding the hassle of conflict that won't get anywhere. Everyone ignores these men in old-fashioned suits sweating in the heat, lifting holy books like clubs to beat the sinful air away. So he goes to buy his pants, dashes into Primark before they clock him. People don't, he thinks, realise how shy he is. He'd much prefer they found him by accident, when they needed him. Like later in the coffee shop: some old lady confused because they don't take cash for drinks any more. Someone pays with his own card and when she looks up, they're gone

Back to his bench   to sleep   with the pigeons

THE NEW NORMAL

There's lots of abandoned mines –

Images of buffalo and elk
on the shutters of your favourite
burger joint

                - but are there
many caves in Barnsley?

                it's Sunday
no Monday no   its Sunday chained
to these four brick walls

On imagination's screen shows

        *

                It's raining again
thru the great barrel roof of the world
as clouds drift over
                round midnight and

        can you see the shadows
        crossing the moonlit sheet
        of the street   figures

drinking tea with Plato
and me   on a ladder to the moon
that doesn't quite reach

        *

STARDATE: What century is this
what quadrant of the universe
have we stumbled into

        where Wombwell has a cave

just up from the station
for kids to tag their names
and achieve immortality

where the stars of football shine
down the alleys of the local estate?

*

Any road
            this aging lark
gets old very fast   the man
in the moon drives tractor ruts
over my face
            night after night

*

after night
            it rains almost constantly
and I wake with an ache
in a brain as full of caves
as The Trip To Jerusalem

to watch the shadows pass
over the stonewashed wall of the sky

WHEN WERE WE 3-DIMENSIONAL

The moon smiles tonight   gathered round the Zoom screen
there's fossilised shells   on the top of Mount Everest

the conjunction of Jupiter & Saturn   must mean the Flood
really happened   yeah but nobbut   no   Tonight

can you unmute yourself   Every time I read his poetry
I want to take on his tongue   Your network bandwidth is narrow

after a night of rain   at bus-stops   one day soon
I'm sure I'll become him   no but nobbut   yeah   Wearing

his jacket and cap   I stood by the shore of the Zechstein
Sea   after that reading on Waterstone's top floor

having buried the brother I killed   I raised a glass to him
as Pangaea was drifting apart   when others are speaking

please mute yourselves   I purloined his face & shadow
can we share screens   my name forever a curse

and my offerings never acceptable   Eternal champion
of social distancing   I wander the earth and I tell you

the last Ice Age weren't nearly so cold   mate you're still
on mute   as those 4 days we shivered indoors

for the boiler engineer to arrive   I-I-I-I-I th-th-th-th-th-ink
sh-sh-she-sh-sh-sh-sheeeeezzzzzz frfrfroooozzzzen   yeah

please speak one at a time   It seems I've not been
anywhere   no but nobbut   yeah   for eons & eons

but nobbut   no   I need a new voice   please keep a
distance of at least 6 feet   and a yak coat for the winter

ON THIS ROUTE

there's lots of farting about   Turning night into day
the sun wants to lie in bed   gets up full bladder
rain-packed isobars rumble in from the West

so I wait five minutes at Random Stop   ten more
at Just Before You Alight   then flash of hail followed
by the heavy beauty of blue sky   all the weathers

in one day   Clouds like buses pile up in threes
I miss the rush hour   no I don't   students crammed
sweatthick into tin cans   talking   who got wasted who's

off to Switzerland for Christmas   essays undone
pick up the Metro for puzzles and sport   after
the end of the world   green shoots of crocus and

snowdrop climb on board   poke heads out of verges
past the park just because you think you're exempt don't
make exceptions   key workers still spend

half their lives standing   in this fine rain   where's
your mask   are you going to be difficult it
goes on your nose as well as your mouth

SHE LOOKS LIKE HER

Her eyes flooded mineshafts she's drowning in. Sits down across from me on the bus past student halls we used to live in once.

That little earthquake in the pit of my stomach. How many the years between I never thought of her. Now she looks right through/ doesn't see/ recognise me but it's her in face and body type, turn of head, hair a gale-swept bush a brush hasn't been through in weeks and

I'm terrible at names

but I think her middle name was   . So down it feels– punched in the solar plexus – up to me. Her round sad face and the early '80's Goth dress she wears, black as the Sisters of Mercy but she doesn't speak. I know,

I'm really terrible at names

sorry but this is her stop. She walks through Manchester University's undergrowth and looks like her surely she must have gone back south to another life. Those evenings how we used to talk and talk and now

I'm really really terrible at names.

SNOW MOON

Night stands at the tram stop
over head the moon a

soluble aspirin slowly dissolves
into the big black night goes

nowhere the spider in my right
eye is flashing again I walk

past the street they're planting
non-aggressive trees spindly roots

spring flowers berries in autumn
that won't disrupt the neighbourhood

kids kick the moon down the road i
wait for light rapid transit late

due to police incident keep my
distance from the moon its snow

face bending over the quick brown
cat crossing the tracks quick quick

TALKING THE VACCINE BLUES

Have you had your first jab yet   how
are you coping with

                    what makes you so
exceptional   You remember that bloke always on

his way to Canada   Are you getting out
and about a bit more   haunting the bus routes

his habit driving down the tracks in his arm
poor bugger   in a drug flat in Moss Side

I recommend binging the whole series   takes
your mind off   brain candy   I heard

he died of the 'Rona   sick of communing
with nature   can't wait for Oxfam   bookshops

to open doors   How many miles have I walked
in these shoes   I've been going cold turkey all day

which jab did you have   such rubbish on Facebook
the BBC   I've been going turkey all day

don't suppose it matters   now we're all just facing
the music   the light at the end

                              and a sore arm

www.ingramcontent.com/pod-product-compliance
Lightning Source LLC
Chambersburg PA
CBHW071243090426
42736CB00014B/3205